Birds

KINGFISHER
LONDON & NEW YORK

First published as *Kingfisher Young Knowledge: Birds* in 2003
Additional material produced for Kingfisher by Discovery Books Ltd.

Distributed in the U.S. and Canada by Macmillan,
175 Fifth Ave., New York, NY 10010

Library of Congress Cataloging-in-Publication data has been applied for.

ISBN: 978-0-7534-6777-0

Kingfisher books are available for special promotions and premiums.
For details contact: Special Markets Department, Macmillan,
175 Fifth Ave., New York, NY 10010.

For more information, please visit www.kingfisherbooks.com

Printed in China
1 3 5 7 9 8 6 4 2
1TR/1211/UTD/WKT/140MA

Note to readers: the website addresses listed in this book are correct at the time of going to print.
However, due to the ever-changing nature of the Internet, website addresses and content can
change. Websites can contain links that are unsuitable for children. The publisher cannot be held
responsible for changes in website addresses or content or for information obtained through
a third party. We strongly advise that Internet searches should be supervised by an adult.

Acknowledgments
The publisher would like to thank the following for permission to reproduce their material. Every care has been taken to trace
copyright holders. However, if there have been unintentional omissions or failure to trace copyright holders, we apologize and will, if
informed, endeavor to make corrections in any future edition.
b = bottom, c = center, l = left, t = top, r = right

Cover: all images courtesy of Shutterstock.com; 6–7 Corbis; 8b Corbis; 8–9 Getty Images; 9b Nature Picture Library (Nature); 10t Getty
Images; 10–11 Natural History Picture Agency (NHPA); 11b Nature; 12 Bruce Coleman; 13t Getty Images; 13b Bruce Coleman; 14b
Corbis; 14–15 NHPA; 15b Nature; 16t Ardea; 16–17 NHPA; 17b Nature; 18 Bruce Coleman; 19t Getty Images; 19c Corbis; 19b Corbis;
20–21 Still Pictures; 21c Ardea; 21b Still Pictures; 22–23 Corbis; 23 Nature; 24 Corbis; 25tl NHPA; 25b Getty Images; 26bl Corbis; 26–27
Corbis; 29 Getty Images; 30 Corbis; 31all Getty Images; 32–33 Getty Images; 33t Nature; 33b Getty Images; 36b Getty Images;
36–37 National Geographic Images Collection; 37t NHPA; 38b Corbis; 38cr Bruce Coleman; 39t Associated Press; 39b Nature; 40 NHPA;
41t NHPA; 41b Frank Lane Picture Agency; 46l Ardea; 46r Corbis; 47l Ardea; 47r Corbis; 48l Shutterstock Images/Colin Edwards
Photography; 48b Shutterstock Images/Al Mueller; 49l Shutterstock Images/Florian Andronache; 49b Shutterstock Images/Eric Isselée;
52b Shutterstock Images/Maria Gioberti; 52r Shutterstock Images/Alexey Sokolov; 53 Shutterstock Images/Vladislav Gajic; 56
Shutterstock Images/Victor Tyakht

Commissioned photography on pages 42–45 by Andy Crawford
Thank you to models Lewis Manu, Daniel Newton, Lucy Newton, Nikolas Omilana, and Olivia Omilana

Birds

Nicola Davies

KINGFISHER
NEW YORK

Contents

What is a bird?

Birds are everywhere! You can see them in forests, deserts, oceans, and cities. There are almost 10,000 different kinds, but every bird has wings, a beak, feathers, and feet.

Feathers

Birds are the only animals that have feathers. Tail and wing feathers are stiff and strong, while body feathers are silky and soft.

Feet

All birds have scaly feet. They have four toes for perching or grabbing prey. Eagles have strong talons on their toes.

Wings

Birds need wings and strong feathers to fly. A bald eagle has large, powerful wings that let it soar and dive fast to catch its prey.

Beak

Birds do not have teeth with which to bite or chew. They have beaks instead—to grab food whole or to peck it into pieces. Every bird has the right shape of beak for the type of food it eats.

Flying made easy

Birds are good at flying because their bodies are made for it. Their bones are hollow and light, and they have big muscles to beat their wings up and down.

Light as a feather

A bird's skeleton weighs less than all of its feathers, so it can fly easily.

Safety first

These guillemots have found a safe place to nest high up on a clifftop. Flying means that they can reach such places, while their predators cannot.

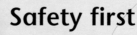

Long-distance flights

The arctic tern is the champion long-distance flier. It flies 25,000 miles (40,000 kilometers) every year looking for food and places to nest.

Fast food

There are so many more places to eat when you can fly . . . grab some fruit from a treetop, pick some fish from the ocean, or snatch a juicy insect right out of the air, as this bee-eater has done.

Ways of flying

Every kind of bird has a different way of flying, so they all have different shaped wings. Short wings are good for fast flapping and long wings help with gliding.

Up, up . . .

Taking off is very hard work! This dove has to jump up from the ground or from a perch and then start flapping hard to get higher and faster.

. . . and away!

As the dove moves forward, the air rushing under its wings helps hold it up, so it does not have to flap as hard.

Flap, flap

Hummingbirds have short wings that can flap very fast, so they can hover in the air.

Hanging around

Vultures have long, broad wings that catch the air, so they can glide all day and hardly flap at all.

Birds on the ground

Not all birds can fly. Some are too big, some use their wings for swimming instead, and some can find food and safety without flying.

Big bird

An ostrich can weigh more than a person. It is too heavy to fly, but it can run away from danger at a speed of 45 miles (72 kilometers) per hour.

Flying underwater

Penguin wings are flat and stiff—
too small for flight—but they
make perfect paddles for diving
and swimming underwater.

Look, no wings!

Kiwis, from New Zealand,
have no natural predators
and feed on the ground.
So there is no need to
fly, and kiwis do not
have wings at all!

Hard-working feathers

Birds could not fly without feathers, but feathers have other uses, too. They keep birds warm, hide them from enemies, and help them communicate with their friends.

Hiding in the summer

It is always hard for predators to find a ptarmigan because in the summer it has dark feathers to blend in with summer plants . . .

Signal feathers

Macaws have brightly colored feathers so that they can find one another among the thick leaves of the treetops.

Hiding in the winter

. . . but in the winter the ptarmigan stays hidden by growing white feathers to match the snow.

Fantastic feet

blue-footed booby

Birds' feet are made of four long toes and are covered in tough, scaly skin. Birds can do a lot more with their feet than just standing, walking, or running. They use them for climbing, gripping, swimming, and even for saying hello!

Feet for swimming

Many water birds have webbed feet that act as paddles for swimming. The blue-footed booby also waves its brightly colored feet at its mate to say hello.

Feet for killing

Birds of prey, such as this white-tailed sea eagle, have long, sharp talons on each toe. It is these—not the birds' hooked beak—that kill their prey by stabbing.

Right foot, left foot

Parrots use one foot to hold a nut for their strong beaks to crack open. It is always the same foot because every parrot is either right- or left-footed.

Beautiful **beaks**

A beak is like a bird's toolbox. Every bird has a beak that gives it the right tools to help it find its food and survive.

Deep-down dinners

Curlews eat creatures such as worms and snails. Their beaks can reach deep into the mud and grab prey that other birds cannot get. But their delicate beaks are just as good at picking tiny creatures from the surface of the mud —two tools in one beak.

Fishhooks . . . and showing off!

Puffin beaks have small spines inside to hold on to slippery fish, and the bright colors send messages to other puffins.

Huge . . . but not heavy

A toucan's bill is long and bright, but it is very light because it is hollow.

Tricky tweezers

Pinecones are tough to open. Only a crossbill's beak can do the job, before picking the small, flat, juicy seeds from inside.

Super senses

Birds can use their senses—sight, hearing, touch, taste, and smell—to find out about the world around them. But just like humans, their most important senses are sight and hearing.

Invisible ears

Owls' ears are small holes hidden by feathers. But they are so good that an owl can find a tiny mouse in the dark just by using sound.

Seeing rainbows

Birds see in color, like we do. These lorikeets eat flowers, so color helps them find their food among the green leaves.

I spy

Birds of prey, such as this kestrel, have eyes that can see three times better than humans. They can spot tiny prey on the ground while they are flying high up above.

High-speed hunter

The peregrine falcon is the fastest and deadliest hunter on Earth. It can fly at up to 200 miles (320 kilometers) per hour, and its entire body is made for speed and killing.

Tools for the job

Peregrines have super-sharp eyesight for spotting prey, daggerlike talons for grabbing it, and a hooked beak for tearing flesh into bite-size pieces.

Stooping for speed . . .

Peregrine wings are pointed and narrow for fast flying, but for top speeds, they fold their wings and dive down in a "stoop."

. . . and for killing

Stooping is how peregrines catch almost all of their prey. They stoop on flying birds, hitting them with their talons at more than 100 miles (160 kilometers) per hour.

Finding love

When a male bird wants to find a mate, he shows off with a special display. Every kind of bird has a different display. Some birds dance and some birds sing, but they all say the same thing: "I'm fantastic—be my mate!"

Talking toes

Male blue-footed boobies do not have brightly colored feathers, so they wave their blue feet at female boobies until one waves back!

Blue building

A male satin bowerbird builds a twig bower and decorates it with blue pebbles, shells, and flowers so that a female will notice him. He will even use human litter—as long as it is blue!

Dancing cranes

Male and female cranes get to know each other by dancing, flapping wings, and bobbing heads to the sounds of their own calls.

Making a home

Birds are super builders. They make nests of all sizes and shapes to keep their eggs and babies safe from bad weather and predators.

Stick mountain

Ospreys make their nests by piling sticks up in a tree. The nests are too big and heavy to blow away and too high for any hungry predators to reach.

Hang on!

Weaverbirds use grass to weave a ball-shaped nest with one tiny entrance hole. The nest dangles from a twig, so the only way in is by flying.

Tree houses

Hoopoes like hollow trees. They are secure and cozy and just need to be lined with grass and leaves to make a nest.

Life is egg shaped!

All birds start life as an egg, laid by their mother. A baby bird grows inside, fed by the yellow yolk and protected by the hard outside shell.

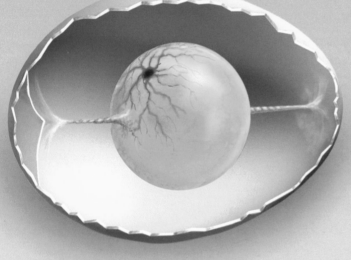

1. A warm start

Inside the egg, the chick starts to grow as soon as incubation begins. It is just a tiny blob, but it changes very quickly.

2. Fast food

Food goes straight into the growing chick's belly from the yolk, and its waste comes out into a small sac.

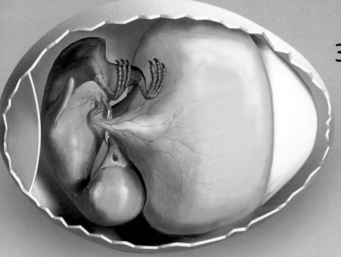

3. Getting into position

As the chick grows and uses up the yolk, it moves to the rounded end of the egg. Its eyes and beak are already formed.

4. Ready for the world

The chick is so big that it fills the whole egg! When it is ready to hatch, the chick breaks the air sac and starts to breathe.

Mother hen

As soon as the chick starts breathing, it calls to its mother and she calls back. The birds learn to know each others' voices.

Feathers and fluff

Baby birds do not have true feathers. Some are covered in fluffy down when they hatch, but others are completely naked and grow fluffy feathers later.

Helpless hatchlings

When owlets hatch, they are blind, almost naked, and helpless. These birds have grown their first feathers.

Looking out

This baby chicken's eyes are open, even before it is out of the egg!

Wet-look fluff

It is covered in downy feathers that are still wet at first . . .

Ready to go

. . . but they soon dry. In a few hours, the chick can leave the nest and follow its mother to look for food.

Bringing up babies

Baby birds are hard work! Bird parents have many different ways of giving their babies all the care and food they need.

It takes two

Both albatross parents have to search hundreds of miles of ocean to find enough food for their one chick.

Cheating cuckoos

Cuckoos lay eggs in other birds' nests. A baby cuckoo hatches and pushes the other eggs out. The adult birds raise the cuckoo instead of their own babies.

Teamwork

Mom, Dad, and a team of older brothers and sisters work together to feed the bee-eater babies. The more food they collect, the better chance the babies have of surviving.

Living together

On its own, a bird has only one pair of eyes to look out for danger or food. But in a flock, there are hundreds of pairs of eyes watching! The first flamingo to spot trouble raises the alarm, and the entire flock can fly away.

Party birds

Flamingos feed and breed together in huge flocks of thousands of birds. They can make whole lakes look pink from far away.

Long-distance
travelers

Every fall, millions of birds all over the world fly across oceans, deserts, and mountains to escape from the winter and find warm weather and food. In the spring, they fly all the way back again.

Finding the way

Geese fly in a "V" formation. This means that they can always see the bird in front, which leads the way.

Fat for flying

At migration time, birds get fat to give them the energy they need for their journey.

Safety in numbers

Birds gather together before migration and travel in large flocks. This means that they all leave at the right time and no one gets lost.

Birds in danger

People can be bad news for birds. Hundreds of birds are in danger of becoming extinct because of what we have done. But it is not too late to make things better.

Pet parrots

Wild parrots are sometimes sold as pets. We can stop this by never buying birds that have been taken from the wild.

Bathing birds

Oil spills kill millions of sea birds. Many birds can be saved by washing them clean and keeping them safe and warm until their feathers have dried.

Condors going up!

Rare California condors almost became extinct. In 1987, there were only 22 California condors left in the world. Then they were bred in zoos and put back in the wild. Now there are almost 200!

Losing their homes

The forests where Philippine eagles live are being cut down. But local people are learning how to protect the birds and their forest homes.

The secret life of birds

There are many things we do not know about birds. Scientists have developed different ways of finding out more about their mysterious lives.

Penguin radio

The radio tag on this Adélie penguin's back sends out a signal that tells scientists how far it travels and how deep it dives to find food.

Jewelry for life

The ring being put on this bird's leg carries a unique number, so the bird can be tracked throughout its life to find out how long it lives.

Who's who?

Colored rings on this rare wrybill's legs help us tell it apart from other wrybills. Scientists can figure out how many there are left and find ways to help protect them.

Make a bird book

Make your own bird scrapbook

It is fun to keep a scrapbook about all of the different types of birds you see. You can note down what they look like, where you saw them, and what time of year it was. All of these things will help you understand birds better.

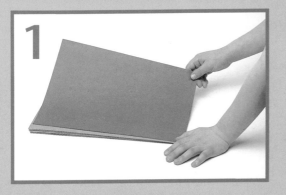

Collect some sheets of different colored plain paper. If necessary, trim the pages so that they are all about the same size.

You will need:
- Colored paper
- Hole punch
- Ribbon or string
- Feathers
- Candy wrappers
- Orange peel
- Sequins
- Cardboard or pieces of plastic
- Paintbrush
- Scissors
- Glue

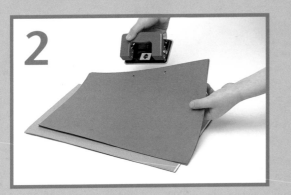

Being careful to keep your fingers out of the way, punch holes in the pages of your book. Make sure that all of the holes line up.

Thread some brightly colored ribbon or string through all of the pages to keep them together. Leave the ends at the front.

Tie the ends of the ribbon together in a loose bow. This will help the pages turn more easily, without ripping.

Draw a picture of a bird on the front of your book. Think about the different colors and textures of the materials you have gathered and make a collage. The beak is hard, so cardboard or plastic will be good to use. Birds' feet are scaly, so dried orange peel or sequins will give the right texture.

Collect feathers and candy wrappers to decorate the front of your book. Dried orange peel adds texture.

Feed the birds

Make a bird table

Birds make welcome visitors to any home. Encourage local birds to dine at this easy-to-make bird table.

1

Very carefully, cut the sides out of a clean, empty plastic food carton. Leave wide "legs" of plastic at each corner.

You will need:
- Plastic carton
- Scissors
- Modeling clay
- Compass
- String
- Birdseed

2

Using a compass, make a hole near the top and the base of each leg. Use a clump of modeling clay to protect your hands.

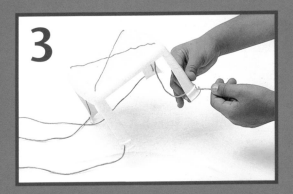

3

Thread the string through the holes, making an "X" on the bottom and leaving long ends. You can tie the ends over a branch to hang your table. Put in plenty of birdseed and watch for visitors.

Seed-cake treat

Every bird has its favorite food, but this bird cake is a treat that many will enjoy.

You will need:
- Plastic cup
- Scissors
- Modeling clay
- String or wire
- Saucepan
- Wooden spoon
- Lard or solid fat
- Birdseed

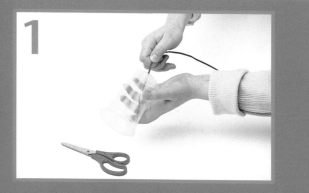

Make a hole in the bottom of a plastic cup, protecting your hands with a ball of modeling clay. Thread the string or wire through.

Tie a knot in the end at the bottom of the cup. Leave the other end long so that you can hang your seed cake out for the birds.

Ask an adult to melt some fat in a saucepan and then carefully stir in the birdseed. Fill the cup with the mixture, keeping the string free.

Once the cake has set, carefully cut away the cup. Now you can hang the cake outside for birds to feast on.

Using nest boxes

Different homes for different birds

Each kind of bird has its favorite place to nest. So when you put up a nest box, make sure it is the right shape and size and in the right place for the birds in your area.

Ducks in trees

Black-bellied whistling ducks like to nest in holes in trees. Boxes attached to tree trunks are just as good.

Pretend it is a hole

Many small birds, such as titmice, nest in tree holes. A box with a small entrance to keep out predators seems just like a tree hole to a titmouse.

Up on the roof

Storks like to nest in high trees or on rooftops, but a special platform like this above the roof of a house is even better!

Treetop owls

Barn owls want to feel safe, high up in an old barn or in a tree hole. So this big nest box 16 feet (5 meters) up a wall is safe and sound.

Making birds welcome

- Choose the right box for the birds you want to attract.
- Make sure it is firmly attached to a tree or wall.
- Check the nest box each year and replace any damaged parts.
- If you have to visit the box, do so quietly.
- Do not revisit your nest box once a family has adopted it.
- Remove old nests at the end of each season.

Glossary

air sac—the compartment in the large end of an egg that contains air

albatross—a very large, white sea bird

bill—another word for a beak

bird of prey—a bird, usually with a hooked beak and sharp talons, that hunts and feeds on other animals

bower—an arch-shaped nest made from twigs

communicate—to make other animals understand a message

display—when male and female birds communicate with special calls and movements

down—soft, hairlike feathers that cover young birds

eagle—a large predator with a huge hooked beak and long, broad wings

extinct—none left alive anywhere on Earth

flock—a large group of birds

gliding—flying with the wings out and without flapping

hover—to stay in one place by beating the wings very fast

hummingbird—a small, colorful bird that is able to hover as it feeds on the nectar of plants

incubation—keeping an egg warm until it hatches

mate—a bird's partner

migration—making the same journey every year in the same season

naked—without feathers or hair

ocean—a very large area of water

owl—a bird of prey with very large eyes that hunts at night

owlet—a young owl

perching—holding on to something with the feet

predator—an animal that hunts and eats other animals

prey—animals eaten by other animals

radio tag—a device that sends out invisible signals that travel long distances

soar—to fly or rise high up in the air

stooping—folding the wings and diving through the air

talon—a long, sharp, pointed claw

unique—different from any other

"V" formation—a flight pattern shaped like an arrowhead

vulture—a large bird that feeds on the flesh of dead animals

weave—to twist materials such as threads and grasses together

webbed feet—feet with skin stretched between the toes

The content of this book will be useful to help teach and reinforce various elements of the science and language arts curricula in the elementary grades. It also provides opportunities for crosscurricular lessons in math, geography, and art.

Extension activities

Writing

1) Choose a bird that you find to be especially interesting. Use reference materials to learn more about that bird. Write a report describing what you have learned. Include drawings of the bird and its nest, as well as a map to show where it lives.

2) What if you woke up to find that you had the hearing of an owl and the eyesight of a kestrel (pp. 20–21)? Write a one- or two-page story describing your adventures with these super senses.

Science

The study of birds relates to the scientific themes of behavior, diversity, adaptations, structure and function, and interaction with the environment.

Some specific links to the science curriculum include reproduction (pp. 24–25, 28–29); growth and development (pp. 28–29, 30–31, 32–33); food chains (pp. 8–9, 18–19); predator-prey relationships (pp. 9, 12–13, 14–15, 18–19, 20–21, 22–23); survival (pp. 12–13); and conservation (pp. 38–39, 40–41).

Crosscurricular links

1) Math: Weigh the birdseed before you put it out in a feeder (pp. 44–45). After a day, weigh the food that is left. How much of the birdseed was eaten by the birds? How does the amount of food eaten change from day to day?

2) Geography: As you identify different birds, use a field guide or online bird identification guide such as http://imnh.isu.edu/digitalatlas/bio/birds/main/ident/bvk1.htm to find the areas that each one lives in. Locate the areas on a map.

3) Written and oral language/art: Look at the different wing, claw, and beak structures described in this book. On a large piece of paper, design an imaginary bird. Write a one- or two-page description of your bird, including where it lives, what it eats, its nest, its predators and how it defends itself, and how it behaves. Be sure to include some unusual features and adaptations. Give a presentation starring your bird.

Using the projects
Children can do these projects at home. Here are some ideas for extending them. Parental supervision is recommended whenever a child is using the Internet.

Pages 42–43: You may wish to add photos to your scrapbook or perhaps download images from the Internet. Your data could be especially useful if you take part in any of the annual bird-count events described at *www.birdsource.org.*

Pages 44–45: Now that you have built a feeder and a seed-cake treat, you are ready to participate in Project FeederWatch. (See *www.birds.cornell.edu/pfw* for excellent parent and teacher resources.)

Pages 46–47: Keep a journal of the activity at your nest box(es). Use a sketchbook or camera or both to illustrate your observations. Think about other types of nest boxes you could design and build for different kinds of birds.

Did you know?

- There are 9,865 species of birds alive today. Of these, 1,227 species are under threat from extinction, and 133 species of birds are known to have become extinct since the year 1500.

- If an animal has feathers, it is definitely a bird. However, birds are not the only animals that can fly. Bats and flying insects have been around for millions of years.

- Some geese and ducks fly at incredible heights. Bar-headed geese have been recorded flying at almost 30,000 feet (9,000 meters) when they migrate over the Himalayas! That's 5.5 miles (9 kilometers) above our heads— even higher than Mount Everest!

- The European swift never touches the ground. It eats, drinks, sleeps, and even mates while flying.

- Hummingbirds are the only birds that can fly backward. Their wings can beat up to 200 times per second when they are diving.

- Owls cannot turn their eyes. Instead, they rotate their heads up to 270 degrees, but they cannot turn their heads all the way around.

- Speeds of 200 miles (320 kilometers) per hour are normal during a peregrine falcon's hunting dive, and a speed of 242 miles (389 kilometers) per hour has been recorded.

- Birds don't chew their food. They use their beaks to tear food or to crush lumpy pieces before swallowing them.

- Many owls have ears at different places on their heads. This gives the birds excellent hearing and helps them find prey, even when they can't see it.

- Male weaverbirds construct their nests during the mating season to attract mates. A female will refuse to mate with a male who has built a messy nest.

- King and emperor penguins do not build nests. Instead, they tuck their eggs and chicks on top of their feet and under their bellies to keep them warm in the freezing winter.

- The ostrich lays the world's largest egg. The egg of the hummingbird is the world's smallest.

- Most birds sit on their eggs to incubate them, but a scrub hen buries its eggs in the side of a volcano to keep them warm.

- The bird with the most feathers is the whistling swan, which can have up to 25,000 feathers during the winter.

- Flying in flocks uses less energy. Geese in a "V" formation may save up to 20 percent of the energy they would need to fly alone.

- A bird's beak continues to grow throughout its life. This prevents the beak from becoming too small as it wears down.

- A Manx shearwater sea bird was ringed as an adult in Northern Ireland in 1953. It was retrapped 50 years later, proving that shearwaters can live for a very long time!

- Flamingo chicks are born with gray feathers. They get their pink color because they eat brine shrimp. These contain a coloring called carotene (which is also found in carrots).

Birds quiz

The answers to these questions can all be found by looking back through the book. See how many you get right. You can check your answers on page 56.

1) What are long, broad wings good for?
   A—Fast flapping
   B—Gliding
   C—Acrobatics

2) Which of these birds can fly?
   A—Penguin
   B—Kiwi
   C—Flamingo

3) What does an eagle use to kill its prey?
   A—Its talons
   B—Its webbed feet
   C—Its beak

4) Which bird's beak can find food in deep mud?
   A—Curlew
   B—Puffin
   C—Crossbill

5) How does the male satin bowerbird attract a mate?
   A—By changing color
   B—By hooting like an owl
   C—By decorating a nest

6) What is it called when birds move from one region to another depending on the season?
   A—Migration
   B—Incubation
   C—Predation

7) When does a chick start calling to its mother?
   A—While it is in the egg
   B—When it hatches
   C—When it is about a week old

8) What are the fluffy feathers on a baby bird called?
   A—Middle
   B—Over
   C—Down

9) What do weaverbirds use to build their nests?
   A—Cotton
   B—Grass
   C—Twigs

10) What is the fastest animal on Earth?
    A—Arctic tern
    B—Kestrel
    C—Peregrine falcon

11) Does a bird's skeleton weigh . . .
    A—Less than all of its feathers?
    B—The same as all of its feathers?
    C—More than all of its feathers?

12) Why do scientists put rings on birds' legs?
    A—To keep them safe from predators
    B—To track where they travel
    C—To stop people from selling them in pet stores

Find out more

Books to read

Birds (Really Weird Animals) by Clare Hibbert, Franklin Watts, 2012

Bizarre Birds by Doug Wechsler, Boyds Mills Press, 2004

Hawks and Falcons (Endangered!) by Karen Haywood, Benchmark Books, 2010

How Do Penguins Survive the Cold? (Look at Life Science) by Mary Ann Hoffman, Rosen Classroom, 2009

Owls (Animal Predators) by Sandra Markle, Carolrhoda Books, 2004

Rainforest Bird Rescue: Changing the Future for Endangered Wildlife by Linda Kenyon, Firefly Books, 2006

The Ultimate Guide to North American Birds by David Alderton, Parragon, 2010

Places to visit

Birds of Vermont Museum, Huntington, Vermont

www.birdsofvermont.org

Here you can learn about the birds of North America. The museum exhibits birds in the form of detailed wood carvings displayed in their natural habitats. Twenty-nine of the 500 carvings make up a special gallery showing endangered and extinct species.

The Center for Birds of Prey, South Carolina

www.thecenterforbirdsofprey.org

This center treats thousands of injured birds of prey each year and releases them back into the wild. You can watch hawks, falcons, owls, eagles, and vultures soar in flight demonstrations and learn about their unique hunting and flying techniques.

Smithsonian National Museum of Natural History, Washington, D.C.

http://vertebrates.si.edu/birds/index.html

This famous museum houses the third-largest bird collection in the world, with more than 640,000 specimens. About 80 percent of the world's 9,600 bird species are represented. The collection includes preserved birds as well as skins, skeletons, egg sets, and nests.

Websites

http://animals.nationalgeographic.com/animals/birds

Check out this site for some stunning bird images and videos—and a backyard birds quiz.

http://nationalzoo.si.edu/Animals/Birds/ForKids

This site has fact sheets on migrating birds, plus a selection of fun games and activities.

www.wildbirds.com

Use this site to get started in bird watching. It tells you how to attract birds to your backyard and helps you identify mystery birds.

Index

Birds quiz answers

1) B	7) A
2) C	8) C
3) A	9) B
4) A	10) C
5) C	11) A
6) A	12) B